Date: 1/19/16

A Beginning-to-Read Book

Christmas

by Mary Lindeen

NORWOOD HOUSE  PRESS

DEAR CAREGIVER, The *Beginning to Read—Read and Discover* books provide emergent readers the opportunity to explore the world through nonfiction while building early reading skills. The text integrates both common sight words and content vocabulary. These key words are featured on lists provided at the back of the book to help your child expand his or her sight word recognition, which helps build reading fluency. The content words expand vocabulary and support comprehension.

Nonfiction text is any text that is factual. The Common Core State Standards call for an increase in the amount of informational text reading among students. The Standards aim to promote college and career readiness among students. Preparation for college and career endeavors requires proficiency in reading complex informational texts in a variety of content areas. You can help your child build a foundation by introducing nonfiction early. To further support the CCSS, you will find Reading Reinforcement activities at the back of the book that are aligned to these Standards.

Above all, the most important part of the reading experience is to have fun and enjoy it!

Sincerely,

Shannon Cannon

Shannon Cannon, Ph.D.
Literacy Consultant

Norwood House Press • P.O. Box 316598 • Chicago, Illinois 60631
For more information about Norwood House Press please visit our website at
www.norwoodhousepress.com or call 866-565-2900.
© 2016 Norwood House Press. Beginning-to-Read™ is a trademark of Norwood House Press.
All rights reserved. No part of this book may be reproduced or utilized in any form or by any
means without written permission from the publisher.

Editor: Judy Kentor Schmauss
Designer: Lindaanne Donohoe

Photo Credits:

Shutterstock, cover, 1, 3, 4-5, 6-7, 8-9, 10, 11, 12-13, 14-15, 16-17, 18-19, 22, 23, 24-25, 26-27; Deamstime, 20-21 (©Keeweeboy), 28-29 (©monkeybusinessimages)

Library of Congress Cataloging-in-Publication Data

Lindeen, Mary.
 Christmas / by Mary Lindeen.
    pages cm. – (A beginning to read book)
 Summary: "Learn about Christmas traditions and symbols, including decorating trees,
putting up lights, singing carols, giving gifts, candy canes, Santa, and more. This title
includes reading activities and a word list"– Provided by publisher.
  ISBN 978-1-59953-690-3 (library edition : alk. paper)
  ISBN 978-1-60357-775-5 (ebook)
  1. Christmas–Juvenile literature. I. Title.
 GT4985.5.L56 2015
 394.2663–dc23
                                                      2014047624

Manufactured in the United States of America in Stevens Point, Wisconsin. 275N-062015

Christmas is a special day in the winter.

It is always on the same date in December.

Some people
decorate for
Christmas.

They decorate
inside.

Some people decorate outside, too.

Look at all of the lights!

Some people put
up trees.

They put on lights.

They decorate
the trees.

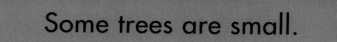

Some trees are small.

Some trees are big!

What is under this tree?

These gifts are Christmas presents.

Red and green are
Christmas colors.

What red and green
things do you see?

These big flowers
are red and green.

They make
good Christmas
decorations.

Candy canes are red and white.

They are a special Christmas treat.

These cookies are also a special Christmas treat.

What colors do you see?

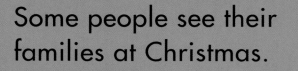

Some people see their
families at Christmas.

Some people sing special
songs called carols.

Do you know who
this is?

It is Santa!

You can see Santa
only at Christmas
time.

Dear Santa?? I

How are you.

Here is what I

Christmas

You can ask Santa
for a present.

Tell him what you
would like.

It is Christmas Day.

Time to open the gifts!

Merry Christmas!

✦ **Reading Reinforcement** ✦

CRAFT AND STRUCTURE

To check your child's understanding of this book, recreate the following diagram on a sheet of paper. Read the book with your child, and then help him or her fill in the diagram using what they learned. Work together to identify examples of Christmas activities, decorations, and colors from this book.

Activities	• • •
Decorations	• • •
Colors	• • •

VOCABULARY: Learning Content Words

Content words are words that are specific to a particular topic. All of the content words for this book can be found on page 32. Use some or all of these content words to complete one or more of the following activities:

- Ask your child questions that include one or more of the content words. Each question should begin with one of these words: who, what, when, where, why, or how.

- Help your child make up sentences that use two or more content words.

- Help your child use content words to make up similes (using the word like or as to make a comparison); for example, It was like night in the tunnel or The tunnel was as dark as night.

- Make up a story together using as many of the content words as you can.

- Help your child make word cards: On each card, have him or her write a content word, draw a picture to illustrate the word, and write a sentence using the word.

FOUNDATIONAL SKILLS: Consonant blends

Consonant blends are groups of two or three consonants that are blended together when pronounced, with each consonant being heard in the blend (for example, *bl* and *nd* as in *blend*). Have your child identify the words with consonant blends in the list below. Then help your child find words with consonant blends in this book.

flowers	green	trees
merry	open	present
families	treat	decorate

CLOSE READING OF INFORMATIONAL TEXT

Close reading helps children comprehend text. It includes reading a text, discussing it with others, and answering questions about it. Use these questions to discuss this book with your child:

- Why do you think people decorate for Christmas?
- What are two Christmas colors?
- What is a special treat to eat at Christmas?
- What is a carol?
- When is Christmas celebrated?
- What can you find under a Christmas tree?

FLUENCY

Fluency is the ability to read accurately with speed and expression. Help your child practice fluency by using one or more of the following activities:

- Reread this book to your child at least two times while he or she uses a finger to track each word as you read it.
- Read the first sentence aloud. Then have your child reread the sentence with you. Continue until you have finished this book.
- Ask your child to read aloud the words they know on each page of this book. (Your child will learn additional words with subsequent readings.)
- Have your child practice reading this book several times to improve accuracy, rate, and expression.

··· Word List ···

Christmas uses the 77 words listed below. *High-frequency* words are those words that are used most often in the English language. They are sometimes referred to as sight words because children need to learn to recognize them automatically when they read. *Content words* are any words specific to a particular topic. Regular practice reading these words will enhance your child's ability to read with greater fluency and comprehension.

High-Frequency Words

a	can	like	small	to
all	day	look	some	too
also	do	make	tell	under
always	for	of	the	up
and	good	on	their	what
are	him	only	these	who
ask	in	people	they	would
at	is	put	things	you
big	it	same	this	
called	know	see	time	

Content Words

candy	date	gifts	outside	special
canes	December	green	present(s)	treat
carols	decorate	inside	red	tree(s)
Christmas	decorations	lights	Santa	white
colors	families	merry	sing	winter
cookies	flowers	open	songs	

··· About the Author

Mary Lindeen is a writer, editor, parent, and former elementary school teacher. She has written more than 100 books for children and edited many more. She specializes in early literacy instruction and books for young readers, especially nonfiction.

··· About the Advisor

Dr. Shannon Cannon is a teacher educator in the School of Education at UC Davis, where she also earned her Ph.D. in Language, Literacy, and Culture. She serves on the clinical faculty, supervising pre-service teachers and teaching elementary methods courses in reading, effective teaching, and teacher action research.